Original title:
Breathing Green

Copyright © 2025 Creative Arts Management OÜ
All rights reserved.

Author: Cassandra Whitaker
ISBN HARDBACK: 978-1-80581-796-3
ISBN PAPERBACK: 978-1-80581-323-1
ISBN EBOOK: 978-1-80581-796-3

The Shade of Renewal

Under the leaves, I sit and sway,
A squirrel scolds me, what can I say?
He says my snacks need more crunch,
I laugh as I munch my leftover lunch.

The grass tickles my toes, oh what a tease,
While dandelions plot, with mischievous ease.
They think they're flowers, all bright and fair,
But really, they just want to mess up my hair!

The breeze whispers tales in my ear,
Of trees that dance, full of cheer.
They say, "Join us, let's have a ball!"
I reply, "I can't even stand up tall!"

Yet here in this shade, all worries flee,
With ants doing salsa and bees set free.
I'll laugh and I'll play till the sun goes down,
In this green-wrapped world, I wear my crown!

Shadows of the Meadow

In the meadow, shadows play,
Tickling daisies, come what may.
A squirrel sneezes, ducks take flight,
Who knew grass could be so bright?

The flowers giggle, petals sway,
A worm recites a joke today.
The sun holds tight to cotton clouds,
While daisies dance in little crowds.

Essence of the Earth

A beetle rolls a giant crumb,
Feasting on a bounty's sum.
A worm declares it's quite a feast,
With tiny friends, they cheer at least.

The soil winks beneath the moon,
While crickets croon their jolly tune.
A dandelion, with winds in tow,
Launches wishes, quite a show!

Melodies of Swaying Grass

The grass is singing, don't you hear?
A jolly tune rings loud and clear.
It sways and twists like dancers do,
Each blade a partner, in green debut.

A rabbit joins, hops to the beat,
As ants march by on tiny feet.
A breeze takes charge, leads the parade,
All join in this grand charade!

Lively Canopy Whispers

Leaves gossip, giggles in the sky,
While branches sway, oh my, oh my!
A crow tells tales of acorn gold,
That daring squirrel, brave and bold.

The sunlight drips, like laughter falls,
On tree trunks warm, where friendship calls.
The canopy's a lively stage,
Where nature's quirks are all the rage!

Hues of Life's Vital Melody

In the garden where giggles grow,
Colors dance in a lively show.
Bees with their buzz sing silly tunes,
While daisies wear hats beneath the moons.

A pumpkin prances with a jolly bounce,
Radishes roll, oh what an ounce!
Lettuce laughs—it's a crispy joke,
Corn's in the corner—just trying to poke.

Vitality in Shades of Grass

Amidst the blades that tickle toes,
A pogo stick once hit a rose.
Frogs in bow ties hop with glee,
Chasing dreams with a cup of tea.

The sunbeam's rays play tag on leaves,
While ants rehearse their funny heaves.
A worm with style shades in the dirt,
Winks at a beetle in a tiny shirt.

A Chorus of Verdant Whispers

When flora chats in the morning light,
Chickens wear glasses—oh what a sight!
Thistles throw parties, they love to twirl,
With daisies and dandelions around to swirl.

Rustling trees crack jokes in the breeze,
While squirrels conduct with style and ease.
A ticklish vine wraps around a stump,
Making all flowers giggle and jump.

The Rebirth of Soft Shadows

In twilight's glow, shadows come to play,
A hedgehog thinks he can dance ballet.
Moss in a hat sips dew with delight,
While fireflies buzz, turning day into night.

An owl in spectacles reads the news,
As rabbits debate their favorite hues.
The breeze claps softly, a gentle cheer,
For all the green antics that bring us near.

Forest's Heartbeat

In the woods, the trees sway,
Whispering secrets night and day.
Squirrels on branches, doing a jig,
While raccoons on logs dance a big gig.

Leaves chuckle in the gentle breeze,
As butterflies float with stunning ease.
Mushrooms laugh, a fungi fest,
What a wild, silly critter quest!

The owls jest with a wink and hoot,
While worms wiggle in their muddy suit.
Nature grins, with a vibrant glow,
In this hilarious forest show!

The Serenade of Sprouts

Little sprouts in the garden groove,
Jigging lightly, in a leafy move.
Dancing flowers, bright and prance,
Tune played by bees makes them twirl and dance.

Worms with top hats wriggle about,
While caterpillars sing, there's no doubt.
Grasshoppers leap with a funny flip,
As ladybugs join this joyful trip.

Raindrops tap like a catchy beat,
Nature's band can't be beat.
Laughter echoing through the green,
In this garden, happiness is seen!

Life's Chlorophyll Dance

Sunlight tickles leaves so bright,
Turning the air into pure delight.
Green socks on the plants have flair,
While daisies dawdle without a care.

The bumblebees buzz a silly tune,
Making the daisies dance 'neath the moon.
Ants march in a comical line,
Each little step feeling quite divine.

Even the ferns twirl in delight,
Playing around, oh what a sight!
Carbon's party, a grand romance,
And everyone's invited to the dance!

Swaying with the Foliage

In the park, the leaves all sway,
With the wind, they frolic and play.
Trees wiggle in their leafy hats,
Squirrels giggle, chasing the rats.

Branches shake with a jolly jig,
While a plump toad sings like a big.
The grass whispers tales so tall,
Nature's laughter is enjoyed by all.

Caterpillars roll into a spin,
Each twist and turn, a laugh within.
Nature's giggles echo loud and clear,
A carnival of greens, we cheer!

Harmony of the Harvest

In fields of corn, I dance with glee,
While bees buzz by, so carefree.
Carrots play hide-and-seek below,
While zucchinis strike a funny show.

Tomatoes blush, feeling quite spry,
As pumpkins plot and squashes sigh.
The harvest sings a quirky tune,
A melody beneath the moon.

Embrace the Leafy Lond

Green hats on heads, we prance around,
In leafy capes, we twirl without a sound.
Frogs in bow ties croak the news,
While worms in shades sip morning brews.

The trees gossip, leaves in flight,
Pinecones giggle, what a sight!
With every shuffle, nature beams,
As laughter joins the swaying dreams.

An Ode to O2

Air so fresh, with a zingy twist,
It lifts my spirits, can't resist.
I blow up balloons filled with cheer,
While oxygen winks, it's crystal clear.

Plants take a breath, join the fun,
They dance in the breeze, just begun.
With every inhale, a chuckle flies,
Nature's punchline beneath the skies.

The Breath of Cypress

Tall cypress trees in a raucous line,
Whispering secrets, feeling divine.
A squirrel with shades, does a wobbly jig,
While pinecones fall, they laugh like a fig.

The breeze brings poems, in leafy flair,
Singing of hugs and trees with hair.
As I giggle with ferns all around,
The forest's humor, forever unbound.

Essence of Summer's Lullaby

The grass has pants, if you can see,
And trees wear hats atop with glee.
Squirrels host dance-offs, what a sight,
Leaves shimmy down to the moonlight.

Buzzing bees, with their tiny tunes,
Chase each other 'round the afternoon.
They wear their stripes, a fashion craze,
Swatting flies in a groovy haze.

Picnics with ants making a fuss,
Stealing crumbs, riding on a bus.
Frogs croak jokes on lily pads bright,
While goldfish giggle, it's pure delight.

So frolic about, join in their cheer,
Summer's here, let's give a cheer!
With humor wrapped in nature's embrace,
Let's dance like grasshoppers, at our own pace.

The Awakening of Flora

Petunias wear shades, totally cool,
Tulips gossip, like they're in school.
Daisies in dresses, twirl with flair,
While sunflowers strike a model's stare.

One might think the flora's shy,
But they throw an annual garden pie!
Roses blushing, with petals so bright,
Hide from daisies, who tease them at night.

The ferns dance wildly, in the soft breeze,
Swinging their fronds with such flair and ease.
Grasshoppers wear ties, oh what a scene,
Caterpillars critique, like they're on a screen.

Watch out for weeds, they crash the show,
Wiggling around, putting on a glow.
Nature's so funny, in all its hues,
Join the chorus, sing these silly blues.

Lush Lyrics

In the park, the popcorn trees,
Pop in the sun, just like a breeze.
Birds belt out their morning tunes,
While squirrels tap dance, to their prunes.

The bushes grumble, all in jest,
Talk about who's the very best.
Rabbits hop to a disco beat,
In this theater, no one's discreet.

Pollen clouds, a tickle fest,
Laughing so hard, the flowers protest.
Bees with bling, in a jewelry shop,
Trading nectar, with a sweet plop!

So grab a seat, it's comedy hour,
In this garden, with nature's power.
A place of giggles, where smiles sprout,
Join the fun, that's what it's about!

Dreams of the Greenbelt

In the greenbelt, dreams take flight,
Olive trees chat, deep in the night.
Cacti debate, who's spikier still,
While llama joins in, with quite the thrill.

Moss makes a pillow, soft and neat,
For woodland critters, it's a cozy seat.
The clouds drift by, with a sly little wink,
While frogs discuss worlds over a drink.

Fireflies flash like disco lights,
As crickets chirp their favorite sights.
A patchwork of laughter fills the air,
Illusions of joy, floating everywhere.

So trek along this verdant scene,
Join the magic, where dreams convene.
Nature's comedy, it's pure delight,
Let's laugh together, under the starlight!

The Green Pulse

In the jungle, I found a frog,
Hopping like a real gym dog.
Chasing flies with goofy grace,
Laughing hard, I join the race.

Trees are holding hands with bees,
Ticklish weeds dance in the breeze.
Swaying grass wants to be a star,
'Take me to the party far!'

Garden of Evocative Breezes

In this garden, gnomes wear shades,
Sunbathing while the sunlight fades.
Flowers giggle in polka dots,
'Who needs water? We need pots!'

Chubby squirrels play hide and seek,
Waving tails, oh, what a peek!
Pansies gossip, tulips tease,
'Let's have fun, forget the bees!'

Fragrant Harmonies in Dappled Light

Daisies strum on dewy strings,
While butterflies flaunt their bling.
A bee with glasses can't quite see,
'Is this petal for you or me?'

The aroma of laughter fills the air,
Pollen parties without a care.
Lavender and thyme in a dance,
Shouting, 'Join us, take a chance!'

Nature's Breath

The hedgehogs wear their funny hats,
Holding court with the chubby bats.
Grass blades whisper jokes at dusk,
'Life's too short, let's have a bust!'

Clouds tickle leaves in their flight,
While crickets host their karaoke night.
Woodpeckers drumming on trees so tall,
'Nature's rhythm, come one, come all!'

Inhale the Forest's Heart

In the woods where squirrels dance,
Leaves do a jig with every glance.
A chipmunk grins, oh what a tease,
While mushrooms giggle in the breeze.

Under green hats, the bugs conspire,
Telling tales that never tire.
With every sniff of pine so tall,
You might just hear a tree's soft call.

Bark's a joker, twisted and sly,
Whispers secrets as you stroll by.
Branches overhead wave hello,
While roots below steal the show.

So take a whiff of nature's prank,
With laughter, nature's spirits rank.
The forest's heart beats loud and clear,
A wacky place, let's give a cheer!

The Liveliness Beneath the Surface

Underneath the leafy cloak,
Worms are laughing, that's the joke.
They're having parties in the dirt,
While crickets chirp in funny shirts.

The skunks are learning how to dance,
Swinging tails in a wild romance.
With every twirl, the mushrooms cheer,
As ants march on like volunteers.

Each puddle's full of froggy tunes,
Ribbiting under the sun's balloons.
A fish might try to wear a hat,
Oh what a sight, imagine that!

So dig a bit, and have some fun,
See the jokes that nature spun.
With every giggle from below,
Life's a circus with a show!

Exhale into Nature's Embrace

Inhale deep, and then exhale,
A squirrel whispers, "Check my tail!"
The trees sway low, oh what a sight,
While busy bees buzz with delight.

The flowers laugh in colors bright,
They strut and sway, what a delight!
With every rustle, leaves will sing,
A tune that only spring can bring.

Breezes tickle as you stroll,
Nature's charm makes you feel whole.
Watch the butterflies parade around,
In silly dances, joy is found.

So let's embrace this lively land,
Where laughter grows just like the sand.
With every step, a chuckle waits,
In nature's realm, it never abates!

Freshness Wrapped in Foliage

Wrapped in green, the world's a treat,
Where dandelions play hopscotch feet.
A rabbit munches on a snack,
While butterflies do acrobat.

Freshness Wrapped in Foliage

The trees wear coats of leafy flair,
As birds drop jokes without a care.
The mossy ground is plush and free,
A trampoline for you and me.

Sunlight tickles through the gaps,
Where creatures nap and take their naps.
The breeze sneezes, pollen flies,
Oh look, a snail in a disguise!

So laugh along with nature's crew,
A silly show, with lots to view.
Amongst the greens, the laughter swells,
In the heart of forest, joy compels!

Exhaling Earth's Lullaby

In the park, I tried to dance,
But tripped on grass and lost my pants.
The trees all laughed, their leaves did shake,
I took a breath — it was a mistake!

The squirrels giggled, what a sight,
As I hid behind a bush, so tight.
I swore I'd never wear those shoes,
Next time I'll stick to my hiking blues!

A dandelion blew me a kiss,
I wondered if nature's had enough of this.
Am I the joke, the comic relief?
With roots so deep, I found my grief.

But in the end, I learned to smile,
I danced with oak, it's worth the while.
With every laugh, the world does spin,
Who knew the trees could be such kin?

Verdant Echoes

A leaf fell gently on my nose,
I sneezed so hard, it made a pose.
The grass beneath began to giggle,
While flowers danced and did a wiggle.

The brook babbled, couldn't keep still,
Told me jokes with every thrill.
I snickered back at nature's puns,
As rabbits raced just for the funs.

A snail with style passed by in style,
Sporting shades and a cheeky smile.
He said, "Take life slow and enjoy the breeze!"
But how could I, as I chased the bees?

So here I stand, amidst the green,
Making friends with every scene.
With trees that talk and clouds so bright,
Nature's humor — pure delight!

The Sigh of the Canopy

In the forest, I took a stroll,
Tripped on roots — oh, what a toll!
The branches swayed and seemed to grin,
"Join the party, come on in!"

A woodpecker knocked like he was DJ,
Beating a tune, come what may.
The mossy floor, a plushy delight,
I flopped down, oh! What a sight!

The breeze whispered, "Why so glum?"
I replied, "Hey, I'm not a bum!"
But laughter echoed among the leaves,
As I wrestled with my tangled sleeves.

So I raised my arms, gave nature a cheer,
And danced with squirrels, loud and clear.
In the canopy, I found my kin,
With every sigh, I joined in the spin!

Verdant Dreams

In my dreams, the grass wore shoes,
And twirled like dancers in the blues.
Bamboo sticks played the saxophone,
While daisies tapped, their talent shown.

A turtle served as DJ, don't you know?
Spinning tracks, putting on a show.
Butterflies flew, choreographed a flight,
In this garden of joy, all felt right.

The clouds wore hats made of fluffy fluff,
While rain drizzled like a watercolor brush.
The moon winked, it was quite a scene,
As I laughed at antics of the green.

But morning came with a jolt and a cheer,
Told my friends, "Join me next year!"
For in those dreams, laughter does bloom,
In fields of joy, let's make more room!

Love Letters to Leaves

Oh, dear leaves, so loud and bright,
You tickle my nose, what a delight!
You dance in the wind, a leafy whirl,
Falling on my head, oh, life's a twirl.

Your green thumbs surely know a trick,
To charm with colors, oh so slick.
Why do you flutter and tease me so?
I swear I'm not crying, just don't let go!

Every autumn, you shout goodbye,
As I gather you up and sigh.
I write you letters but you just blow,
Reply with rustling, oh what a show!

With ink of dew, I pen my line,
To leave more matches, please align.
Your giggles echo in my ear,
Time to gather 'round, my leafy dear!

Murmurs of the Meadow

In the meadow, whispers play,
Grass giggles when kids run and sway.
Dandelions make wishes fly,
While butterflies blush in the sky.

Are you ticklish, dear tall stalk?
I swear I heard you giggle and talk.
The bees are buzzing, what's the joke?
With each sweet buzz, the flowers poke.

Hopping frogs sing off-key tunes,
As crickets chat beneath the moons.
Laughter ripples like a gentle stream,
Nature's humor, a joyful dream!

Oh meadow, you're my happy place,
With every misstep, I find my grace.
Your whispers tickle, make me grin,
In this wild world, where fun begins!

Guardians of Growth

Big brown trees with your barky hugs,
Standing tall like playful bugs.
Your branches wave, give me a cheer,
Whispering secrets only we hear.

In the garden, we dance real slow,
Twirling flowers put on a show.
Why do you bloom in such bright hues?
Oh Snapdragons, what's your excuse?

Watering cans laugh quite a lot,
As mud pies grow in sun-soaked spots.
These green guardians remind us to play,
Sprout with joy, come what may!

So if you see a dew drop roll,
It's just the grass giving its soul.
In nature's kingdom, sweet delight,
Guardians of giggles, day and night!

Emerald Reverberations

Oh, the emerald waves that shimmer bright,
Like a disco ball in the light.
Leaves tap dance as winds blow sweet,
Nature's rhythm, what a treat!

The bushes chuckle, twigs give a squeak,
Lost in laughter, no need to speak.
Squirrels juggle the acorns around,
Jumping for joy, they must abound!

I hear your echoes, soft and clear,
In a forest of fun, it's all sincere.
Every shuffle, a funny affair,
Even the shadows have tales to share!

So let's frolic through this emerald glow,
With giggles as plentiful as we know.
Nature's laughter forever sings,
In the joy that green scenery brings!

The Dance of Nature's Vitality

In the garden, plants all prance,
They sway around in a leafy dance.
Trees wear shoes of bright green leaves,
While flowers giggle, oh, how they tease.

Roots wiggle like they're quite the pros,
Twirling with joy, nobody knows.
A breeze blows in, a partner to share,
Together they spin, without a care.

The sun's rays tickle each petal's face,
Branches sway like they're in a race.
In this green party, you just might find,
Nature's sense of humor, so well-defined.

Bugs don tiny hats, they join the fun,
Who knew that plants could dance and run?
So next time you stroll through a blooming scene,
Remember, it's a dance, not just routine.

Leaves that Laugh with Light.

Up on the branches, leaves have a chat,
They stick out their tongues, how silly is that?
Shimmering softly in the warm sunlight,
They're trading jokes, what a lively sight!

The sunlight plays tag with shadows below,
Leaves giggle softly, "Oh, what a show!"
One leaf whispers, "Hey, look at me!"
I'm flipping and flopping, wild and free!

Pine needles snicker, with a piney grin,
"You call that a dance? Let's spin again!"
The oaks swing low, and the willows sway,
In this leafy circus, all are at play.

Nature's comedians, each has a role,
A punchline hidden in every green bowl.
So join the laughter, let your spirit ignite,
With the leaves that laugh, everything feels right.

Whispers of Verdant Vistas

In fields so bright, with a verdant view,
The daisies gossip, sharing something new.
"Did you see that bee with his fancy flight?"
"Such grace! Such charm! What a hilarious sight!"

The grass blades nod, with a sparkling grin,
"How deep is the drama in the garden kin?"
While trees gossip long about last night's storm,
And how the flowers look in their spring form.

The whispers carry on a gentle breeze,
A ticklish rumor among the trees.
"Did you hear about the sunflower's hat?
So jaunty and bright, it made hearts spat!"

Frogs croak jokes from their muddy seats,
While butterflies turn the sky into sweets.
In this colorful chaos, laughter takes flight,
Whispers of joy in every delight.

Lush Exhalations

In a forest deep where the green things play,
The foliage chuckles, 'Come out, let's sway!'
Each leaf that rustles, a giggle released,
As nature exhales, it seems quite pleased.

The flowers burst forth with a riot of hues,
Telling tales of sunshine and morning dews.
"Hey, look at us! Who needs a song?
Our colors alone will keep you along!"

Froggies hop in their comedy troupe,
With each silly leap, they gather a group.
Their croaks mix like a stand-up spree,
In this lush comedy, who wouldn't agree?

Sunbeams burst forth, like laughter's own light,
Silly shadows dance in delight of the sight.
With nature's embrace, let's let out a cheer,
For the richness of life that surrounds us here!

Fragrant Paths of Serenity

In the garden of socks and old shoes,
A lawn gnome dances, shaking off blues.
With daisies in hand, he starts to prance,
While worms in the dirt giggle and dance!

Buzzy bees wear tiny top hats with flair,
And the daisies' whispers float softly in air.
Squirrels debate on who stole the seed,
As daisies plot a colorful deed!

The ants march in lines like a silly brigade,
While frogs play hopscotch in sun's gentle shade.
Breezes sing ballads of high-flying dreams,
And roses join in with their fragrant screams!

But beware of the garden hose's sly trick,
It sprays unwary feet, oh isn't it slick?
In this silly patch where laughter's the queen,
Life's a big joke, you should sit and glean!

Spirals of the Wild Garden

In a world where tomatoes wear sun hats bright,
And carrots play tag with their roots in flight.
Radishes host parties with rad tunes and snacks,
While cucumbers wobble on their leafy tracks!

The parsley throws shade while the chives all cheer,
As beetles break dance, skimming low to the near.
A sunflower grins, it's got jokes up its sleeve,
While butterflies swoon, it's hard to believe!

The soil whispers tales of the wild and wacky,
As figs play poker, but their hands are quite tacky.
The scent of fresh herbs tickles the nose,
In this spiraled wonder where giggling grows!

Even the rake joins the floral ballet,
Hoping to score points in a quirky display.
With cheer and with chortles, this jungle of cheer,
Reminds us to laugh through the weeds we hold dear!

Life's Vital Essence in Bloom

When daisies decide they want to paint shoes,
And tulips giggle at their colorful hues.
The violets blush, quite shy in their scenes,
While roses just strut in their playful routines!

Lettuce spins tales of a crisp summer breeze,
While squash tells of dreams brought in with the tease.
Cabbages murmur with their leafy green heads,
As the peas crack jokes, though they're often misled!

Each bumblebee dons a bright tuxedo hat,
As they zippity-zap in the moments they chat.
Forget-me-nots giggle, then shyly take flight,
In this circus of life, what a whimsical sight!

So come join the party, don't sit on the fence,
Where every sweet bloom can spark pure suspense.
With petals a-flutter, laughter's the theme,
In this vital orchestra of nature's dream!

Nature's Gentle Respiration

In the forest where ferns hold the giggle-flower,
And mushrooms moonwalk for an hour and hour.
The critters all gather for a splashy parade,
With rabbits in capes and a squirrel masquerade!

The willow weeps laughter, not tears, it is true,
As dandelions cheer, "Come join us! It's you!"
A hedgehog extends his spiky embrace,
To all of the snails who just want to race!

Toads croak their mantras while frogs flip a coin,
As bugs play the banjo, what a strange join!
The breeze carries whispers of giggly delight,
In this playful symphony, all things feel right!

So laugh with the blossoms, they're here for a time,
With nature as humor, it's quite the prime!
In every green hiccup, and twist of the vine,
Let joy be the anthem, so quirky, divine!

Essence of Every Petal

In a garden full of daisies,
The bees hold rigorous meetings,
With buzzing voices, they strategize,
Over sweet pollen and nectar's smiles.

Tulips wear their bright hats tight,
While roses gossip with all their might,
But violets just laugh, carefree and wild,
In this petal party, not one's mild.

Dandelions tumble down the lane,
Playing hopscotch in the sun's warm grain,
A flower's laugh is a bumblebee's dance,
In petals and pollen, we find our chance.

So when you stroll by, don't hold your cheer,
Join in the laughter, come draw near,
For nature's humor is always bright,
In every petal, we're all delight.

Tranquility of the Thicket

In the thicket where squirrels debate,
Who's the best at balancing fate,
They hoard their nuts with giggling sounds,
While birds make jokes from leafy rounds.

The fox considers the local lore,
Of sneaky chipmunks who scamper and score,
While trees sway gently, giggling as one,
Telling the tale of a lost acorn run.

The laughter of leaves is loud and spry,
Who knew branches could giggle so high?
Through rustling whispers, the stories unfold,
Of mischievous critters, both clever and bold.

So take a stroll within nature's prank,
Find yourself grinning, smiling flank to flank,
For in thickets thick with silence and glee,
The best of the jokes are for you and me.

Voices of the Verdant

Under the canopy where fun just thrives,
Each plant shares secrets, in vibrant dives,
With leaves that rustle like giggly friends,
Nature's own laughter that never ends.

Ferns whisper tales of the quirkiest snails,
Who wear tiny hats for their holiday trails,
And daisies tease the forget-me-nots,
For their absent-minded, lost flower thoughts.

In the heart of the field, where grasses compete,
They sway and dance to their own little beat,
A symphony made of rustling good vibes,
Where trees sway together in leafy high fives.

So listen closely, oh curious soul,
Join in the chorus, become part of the whole,
For in every leaf, a narrative's spun,
In the voices of green, laughter has won.

Nature's Silent Invitation

In a meadow where daisies play hide and seek,
Butterflies flutter, with strategies unique,
As whispers of wind carry doubts away,
Each petal's soft giggle, inviting our stay.

The streams babble jokes that only they know,
While the ducks quack out plans for a show,
With reeds involved, comedic flair in sight,
Who knew this green world could be so bright?

Every nook and cranny holds laughter in store,
With critters conspiring, their plots galore,
In the crickets' chorus, a comedy play,
As nature's applause wraps around us today.

So come and join this green-hued ball,
With squirrels as jesters, we're having a ball,
In this silent invitation to chuckle and sing,
We find joy in the quirks that the green world can bring.

Hushed Whispers of Hills

On emerald slopes, the cows do sway,
Mooing secrets in their own way.
Grassy gossip from yon hilltop,
Echoes 'til the daisies stop.

Squirrels plot with acorn plans,
Scheming goofballs in leafy bands.
Twirling leaves in an autumn dance,
While rabbits resume their wild prance.

fresh facades

In gardens where the veggies tease,
Tomatoes giggle in the breeze.
Carrots don their orange pants,
While peas decide to step and prance.

Radishes wear their best attire,
Potatoes dream of being higher.
With every sprout that waves hello,
Nature's jokes are sure to flow.

Life in Every Blade

Blades of grass, oh what a crew,
Doing cartwheels, just for you.
Giggling daisies join the show,
Each leaf is part of the frolic flow.

A worm takes center stage today,
Wiggling wildly, come what may.
In the sunlight, laughter spills,
Nature's antics give us thrills.

Awakening with Nature

At dawn, the flowers stretch and yawn,
Giving sleepy bees a fawn.
Butterflies in silly flight,
Dancing through the morning light.

A wind that tickles every stem,
Plants giggle at their own whim.
The world wakes up to nature's jest,
In this green land, we are blessed.

Whispers of Lush Renewal

In a jungle of sneezes, trees take a bow,
As leaves play hide and seek with a cow.
Frogs croak in rhythm, a green karaoke,
While squirrels throw nuts like confetti—so hokey!

The daisies gossip, the violets giggle,
The bushes perform their best fuzzy wiggle.
With worms in tuxedos, they dance in a line,
It's a wacky affair, nature's own showtime!

Grasshoppers debating if they can fly,
While snails are just chilling, feeling spry.
Bamboo shoots whisper their secrets so sweet,
With roots that are plotting a rootin'-tootin' feat!

In the canopy's cradle, a laughter parade,
Where pinecones are clowns, and mischief's well-played.
Nature's own circus, come one, come all!
Join in the revelry, let's have a ball!

Emerald Exhalations

In the shade of a fern, a sloth takes a nap,
With dreams of a world where he's quick as a chap.
The wind tickles leaves, they giggle and sway,
Let's shout out to nature, it's a wacky day!

A raccoon with manners, wearing a tux,
Eats pizza at midnight, oh what a deluxe!
While daisies in suits practice their bow,
It's a fashion show here, and everyone's wowed!

Bees buzzing tunes, like a wild tambourine,
They dance with the blossoms, creating a scene.
With petals like confetti, all set for a dance,
Who says that the flower can't lead a romance?

Under arches of ivy, the shadows do twirl,
Caterpillars gossip, as the butterflies swirl.
The moss starts a party, the rocks play it cool,
Join in the revelry, it's nature's grand school!

Verdant Echoes of Dawn

In the morning light, the tulips stand tall,
They gossip and giggle, it's a floral ball.
A squirrel in shades, with a nut in each hand,
Is plotting a heist for the best acorn brand!

The pitter-pat raindrops form a tap-dance tune,
Where frogs wear top hats, crooning under the moon.
A dizzying waltz of blades and bugs,
With ladybugs laughing, sharing green hugs.

Cacti do stretches, while ferns shake a leaf,
They're welcoming morning, without any grief.
With roots doing cha-chas beneath the ground,
They shake it all off to their own funky sound!

As clouds puff and pounce in a game of pretend,
The sun cracks a smile; it's the day we defend.
In the heart of the garden, the humor's on spree,
Oh, what fun it is in nature's jubilee!

Sighs of the Leafy Canopy

Up in the branches, a parrot sings loud,
Clad in bright feathers, he's completely unbowed.
He cracks silly jokes to the owls at night,
While the stars take their seats for the comedic delight.

A squirrel in a cape zips from tree to tree,
Declaring, "I'm a hero, just wait and see!"
While acorns are rolling like marbles on trails,
He shouts, "I'm the king of the nutty details!"

The whispers of willows weave stories so sweet,
About bees in the park, competing in heat.
"Buzz like you mean it!" a brave bumble pleas,
As they dance wildly in a honey-brewed breeze!

The forest erupts in a lively ballet,
As creatures unite in their whimsical play.
From branches to roots, every plant joins the spree,
In this leafy gala, oh, come laugh with me!

Cadence of the Rustling Woods

In the woods where squirrels prance,
Trees do a little wiggly dance.
Leaves are giggling in the breeze,
What a riot, oh, if you please!

A twig snaps, oh what a fright!
A rabbit hops, darting in flight.
Mushrooms wear their party hats,
While the deer joke, 'Look at those brats!'

Branches sway, a comical sight,
Caterpillars plotting a flight.
Frogs make sounds like silly drums,
Nature's band fills hearts with hums.

Twilight wraps the trees in jest,
As crickets play, they do their best.
The forest giggles, what a show,
A chuckle that will surely grow!

Chasing the Chlorophyll Dream

In a field where grasses sway,
Little bugs come out to play.
They whisper tales of leafy cakes,
And share the gossip that nature makes.

The sun shines bright, it's quite a clown,
Leaves wear crowns, no one wears a frown.
Bumblebees buzz in funky jams,
Even ants know how to scram!

A snail takes a leap, no, a crawl,
He's racing fast, or so he'll call.
The daisies wink in morning light,
While the daisies dance, oh what a sight!

At dusk, the fireflies bring the bling,
They emit sparkles, oh what zing!
Nature's ready for a wild time,
In the chlorophyll dream, we all rhyme!

The Pulse of the Earth Awaits

The ground hums a quirky tune,
With worms doing the cha-cha in June.
A rock grins wide, it's surely wise,
As ants march by in small disguise.

A tree leans in to share a joke,
"Why did the leaf cross? For the poke!"
The streams giggle as they retreat,
Bouncing boulders dance with their beat.

Clouds roll in, what a fun house!
A snail plays cards with a lazy mouse.
The sun flips pancakes made of light,
While shadows chase in wild delight.

At night, the stars twinkle and tease,
The moon chats low with whispering trees.
The earth grins, for it's a laugh,
Celebrating life on a leafy path!

Aromas of Renewal Dance

In the garden, scents collide,
Flavors mixing, nature's pride.
With roses twirling in a frolic,
Even thyme joins in, so hydraulic!

The daisies laugh, "What's that smell?"
"Oh, just mint having a spell!"
The ladybugs paint on the scene,
While peas giggle, bright and green.

Lavender sways like it's in a waltz,
Scenting air without any faults.
The onions tease with a pungent spell,
While carrots hum, 'Oh do not dwell!'

Aroma dances, it's quite a treat,
With herbs and blooms, a fragrant beat.
Nature's kitchen brews a thrill,
In this joke, there's always a fill!

Flourishing Hues

In the garden, gnomes do dance,
With sneakers on, they take a chance.
Petunias giggle, daisies prance,
While sunflowers wear a sassy glance.

Crickets chirp in funny suits,
While worms play jump rope with their roots.
Butterflies sip on juice so sweet,
And bees buzz by with quickened feet.

Tulips trade their colors bright,
Arguing over who's more tight.
The roses roll their eyes in fun,
As pollen rises, one by one.

So here's to greens that twist and twirl,
In this quirky, leafy world.
Where every leaf's a giggling friend,
In hues that brighten till the end.

Whimsy in the Woods

In the woods, a squirrel jives,
While mushrooms wear their fancy vibes.
A rabbit hops with such delight,
In polka dots, what a sight!

The trees clap hands with every breeze,
As shadows play in playful tease.
A woodpecker drums a funky beat,
While ants throw parties at their feet.

Bunnies bake their carrot pies,
Conspiring 'neath the painted skies.
The creek sings songs both fresh and free,
While frogs croak out their melody.

So wander here and laugh a while,
Enjoy the jest, the quirky style.
In nature's realm, let joy expand,
With whimsy dancing through the land.

Nature's Breath

There's a tickle in the park today,
As leaves discuss their plans to sway.
A quirky breeze brings laughter near,
While daisies drop their petals, cheer!

The ants march proudly in a line,
Swapping jokes over tasty brine.
While the sun shines with a goofy grin,
A sunflower shimmies, pulling kin.

The clouds above wear wobbly hats,
As squirrels tease the friendly cats.
In every nook, a chuckle hides,
Where nature's laugh is truth that guides.

So join the fun, the sights, the tease,
With every rustle of the leaves.
A joyful breeze, the world's own laugh,
In nature's breath, we find our path.

Calming Ferns

Beneath the shade, the ferns convene,
In secret meetings, what a scene!
They whisper tales of olden days,
While breezes chuckle in the haze.

With tendrils curling, oh so sly,
They photobomb a passing fly.
A leafy gale begins to twirl,
As green confetti starts to swirl.

In this quiet space, they share their quirks,
As shadows dance and sunlight lurks.
With every rustle, laughter grows,
Revealing seams in nature's clothes.

So take a seat where calmness reigns,
Among the greens, forget your pains.
With ferns around to crack a smile,
In nature's arms, just stay a while.

Vivid Growth

In a forest bursting with cheer,
Trees stretch high with a grin ear to ear.
Squirrels dance in a leafy parade,
While critters sing tunes in the shade.

The flowers gossip in vibrant hues,
Tickling the breeze with their morning muse.
A dandelion bows, then takes a spin,
As ladybugs laugh, saying, "Let's begin!"

Sunbeams tease as they peek and poke,
While branches waggle in a comical joke.
Nature's comedy plays on repeat,
As bugs tap dance on nature's beat.

Here, all is jolly, the humor's in sight,
With green laughter, what a delightful delight!
Each leaf knows the punchline, oh so well,
In this leafy giggle, all is swell!

Sylvan Fragrance

In the woods where the air smells sweet,
Trees wear perfume on every leaf's feet.
Bees hum a tune, buzzing with flair,
While birds crack jokes that float in the air.

A pinecone slips, doing a tumble,
While flowers snicker, and bees start to rumble.
The woodpecker knocks on a tree's funny bone,
Laughing at echoes that make it feel home.

With blooms that sparkle like disco balls,
And vines that twirl with giggly calls,
Moss tickles toes of those who roam,
In this fragrant place, everyone feels at home.

The breeze whispers tales of delightful surprise,
As leaves shake their heads and roll their eyes.
In this sylvan corner where humor plays,
Nature's punchline brightens up the days!

Renewal of the Leaf

Tiny buds peek out with a grin,
Whispering secrets of where they've been.
Each leaf is a joker, ready to tease,
Playing tag with the wind through the trees.

The sun gives a wink, saying, "Time to grow!"
As sprouts stretch out in a lively show.
Chirps add to the chorus, so funny and loud,
While shadows of giggles collect in a crowd.

Frogs leap for joy, in their bright green attire,
As petals pirouette, never to tire.
Nature's comedy club, all are invited,
With laughter and joy, everyone excited.

The cycle spins 'round, each new leaf a jest,
In a world full of fun, we're all truly blessed.
From bud to bloom, let the laughter run free,
In this renewal, come swing and just be!

Tranquil Canopies

Under the trees where the sunlight plays,
Leaves throw cool shade on warm summer days.
The branches chatter with a whimsical tune,
As squirrels plot mischief beneath the full moon.

Hammocks swing low, with giggles abound,
While chipmunks make sure no loose nuts are found.
A raccoon in sunglasses takes a sweet nap,
Stealing the show in nature's great map.

Clouds drift lazily, painting the skies,
While the grass whispers jokes with a wink and a sigh.
With an orchestra of frogs croaking delight,
This canopy's secret is pure, joyous light.

So come grab a seat in this leafy café,
Where laughter and nature sweep troubles away.
Each branch is a comedian, ready to share,
In tranquil repose, we breathe in the care!

A Tapestry of Herbal Harmony

In a garden full of chives,
Where parsley's trying to survive,
Gherkins dance with wicked glee,
Making pickles out of spree.

Thyme and basil argue loud,
While cilantro stands up proud,
But the sage just rolls its eyes,
And pretends to be surprised.

Oregano tells a tall tale,
Of a pizza cruise by sail,
As rosemary starts to dream,
Of a pasta dinner scheme.

Lavender sips tea with cheer,
While the carrots bloom with fear,
In this scene of spice and jest,
Nature's laughter is the best.

Gentle Currents of Green Light

A sprout once tried to run a race,
But tripped on dirt and lost its place,
The beetroot laughed, and roots did tease,
Saying, "Stay grounded! Bring the breeze!"

In a fussy fern convention hall,
The daisies wore their petals tall,
An earthworm slipped, a wormy plight,
And then they all just laughed in spite.

The mint was minty fresh and slick,
While cabbages were playing tricks,
"Let's roll down this grassy slope!"
Gasps of joy—oh, what a hope!

Amidst the whispers of the leaves,
The flowers shared their silly thieves,
In this patch of fun and glee,
Nature's quirks are wild and free.

The Symphony of Serene Growth

A sunflower plays the tuba loud,
While violets cheer a leafy crowd,
Grasshoppers tap out the beat,
While beetles wiggle on their feet.

The daisies don a polka dot,
And sing of all the funny plots,
As lilacs join in sweet refrain,
Creating music in the grain.

A rabbit joins to dance around,
While ferns get tangled on the ground,
And daisies giggle, losing grace,
As pollen flies—a flower race!

In this concert of delight,
Nature's humor shines so bright,
Each note a giggle from the trees,
In this symphony of breezy ease.

Nature's Breath Beneath the Sky

A tree once told a squirrel bold,
"Your acorn stash is worth its gold!"
But with a shrug, the squirrel said,
"I'll plant it here, then go to bed!"

The clouds drift by, a lazy show,
While blossoms bloom, a vibrant glow,
The wind remarks, "What a nice day,"
And tickles leaves in cheeky play.

A snail insists it's quite the race,
Against a tortoise in the chase,
But when they slip on dewy morn,
They end with laughter newly born.

For under sky both wide and bright,
Nature's humor takes its flight,
In the wild, the joyful stride,
Life's joyous quirks are bona fide.

Life Flourishing in Silent Harmony

In the garden, grass wears a hat,
While daisies giggle, imagine that!
The ants are dancing, with tiny shoes,
While squirrels debate, on the evening news.

A snail zooms by, leaves a shiny trail,
Compares his speed to a tiny whale.
Sunflowers cheer, with their yellow glee,
As worms write poems, beneath a tree.

Bees buzz jokes, in a messy choir,
While butterflies plot to steal the fire.
The earth is laughing, oh what a sight,
In this quirky world, everything's right!

So let us join the joyous spree,
With giggles and winks, come dance with me!
Nature's oddities wrap us tight,
In this happy place, pure delight!

Lush Petals Beneath a Blue Canopy

Beneath a sky of cotton candy,
Petals plot and scheme, oh so dandy!
A rose wears shoes to prove her flair,
While tulips argue who'll take the dare.

Dandelions wish for beauty crowns,
As gardeners dance in silly gowns.
With each blooming laugh, colors collide,
In this wacky world, it's a goofy ride!

Clouds giggle as they watch the show,
While raindrops play tag, to and fro.
Sunshine winks at the bubbling brook,
The frogs are drafting their own cookbook!

The breeze tells tales of mischief and fun,
As petals sway, under the sun.
In nature's embrace, we all can see,
How silly life can truly be!

Aroma of the Green Earth

The scent of green fills the air,
While critters laugh without a care.
Mint tea parties under the sky,
With beetles that sip as they munch on pie.

A whiff of grass, a dash of spice,
The chives have jokes, oh isn't that nice?
As daisies tease about their big blooms,
The world is alive, with giggles and zooms!

Frogs catch whispers in their wet hands,
While the roots hold secrets, like bandstands.
The oak tree chuckles as it thinks through,
How even the moss has a joke or two!

So take a deep whiff of this fragrant cheer,
It's nature's laughter, wrapping you near.
In this playground of scents and delight,
Let's frolic in joy, from morning to night!

Threads of Renewal in the Wind

Whispers of wind spin tales so grand,
As petals flutter, hand in hand.
A leaf takes flight, joins a merry dance,
While trees chuckle, giving nature a chance.

The windsocks giggle, with arms open wide,
While clouds on a stroll take things in stride.
Squirrels plan parties up in the air,
With acorns and pinecones, beyond compare.

Vines gossip lightly, sharing a laugh,
As nature unveils its whimsical path.
In this swirling embrace, life takes a spin,
Fruits of renewal, let the fun begin!

So ride with the breeze, join the delight,
In this tapestry woven with pure light.
The threads of mirth weave through the days,
In this joyful dance, let us all play!

Melodies of Growth

In the garden, a dance takes flight,
Worms twist and twirl, what a sight!
Bees buzz along, a funny tune,
Singing with flowers under the moon.

Chickens cluck in a silly way,
Chasing their tails like kids at play.
Sunshine beams with a goofy grin,
While dirt splatters on the neighbor's chin.

Plants whisper jokes to the air,
In leafy hats, they sing without care.
The tomatoes roll, laughing with glee,
As ants march on in a wobbly spree.

A gnome chuckles, moss in his beard,
Sharing the punchline, everyone cheered!
In this green realm, so cheerful and bright,
Nature's humor is pure delight!

Whispers of the Wilderness

The trees gossip when the wind swings by,
"Did you see that squirrel? Oh my, oh my!"
With acorns flying, it's a nutty show,
As branches shake in laughter's flow.

Frogs leap around, croaking in rhyme,
Hoping to impress the bugs in prime time.
A fox struts in a silly disguise,
While bushes giggle with leafy sighs.

In the pond, fish play peek-a-boo,
Swishing their tails like they just flew.
The reeds dance along to nature's beat,
As the sun bakes the mud, oh what a treat!

Bumbles and crickets orchestrate fun,
While shadows hide what's hardly begun.
Comedy thrives in the wild, don't you see?
In the embrace of green, we're all carefree!

Rhythm of Roots

Roots pull the ground like a dramatic dance,
Twisting and turning, taking a chance.
Beans are competing in races so fast,
With carrots sneaking, they're hoping to last.

A pumpkin rolls over, laughing with pride,
While potatoes play hide-and-seek inside.
The radishes blush with their tops in a flare,
Mischief abounds in this underground lair!

Fungi throw parties, that's what they do,
Dancing with bugs for an audience too.
The rhythm of roots, it's a laugh-fest indeed,
Sprouting joy from the soil, it's what we all need!

So join in the fun, your feet in the dirt,
Where even the weeds sport a playful shirt.
Nature's comedy is alive, oh what glee,
In this whimsical world, come and see!

Leafy Interludes

Leaves flutter down like a playful parade,
Tickling the ground as they jig and fade.
A squirrel in spectacles reads a fine book,
While mushrooms chuckle from each little nook.

Sunlight peeks in, winking with flair,
The daisies tease, saying, "Look at our hair!"
While petunias gossip about the next bloom,
And the tulips are plotting a grand costume!

In every whisper, there's laughter to find,
As vines twist and twirl with a whimsy kind.
A bug parade marches on leaves so huge,
Waving their tiny flags, can't refuse!

Nature's a jester with blooms bright and bold,
With stories of folly that never grow old.
So come share a chuckle, let your spirit beam,
In leafy interludes where joy is supreme!

www.ingramcontent.com/pod-product-compliance
Lightning Source LLC
Chambersburg PA
CBHW070324120526
44590CB00017B/2807